FRIENDS
OF ACPL
3 1833 00596 5865
D1283732

Guess What Grasses Do

GUESS WHAT

grasses DO

Barbara Rinkoff
Illustrated by Beatrice Darwin

Lothrop, Lee & Shepard Co.
New York

To Evelyn Hisz

Printed in the United States of America. Library of Congress Catalog Card Number: 76–177316

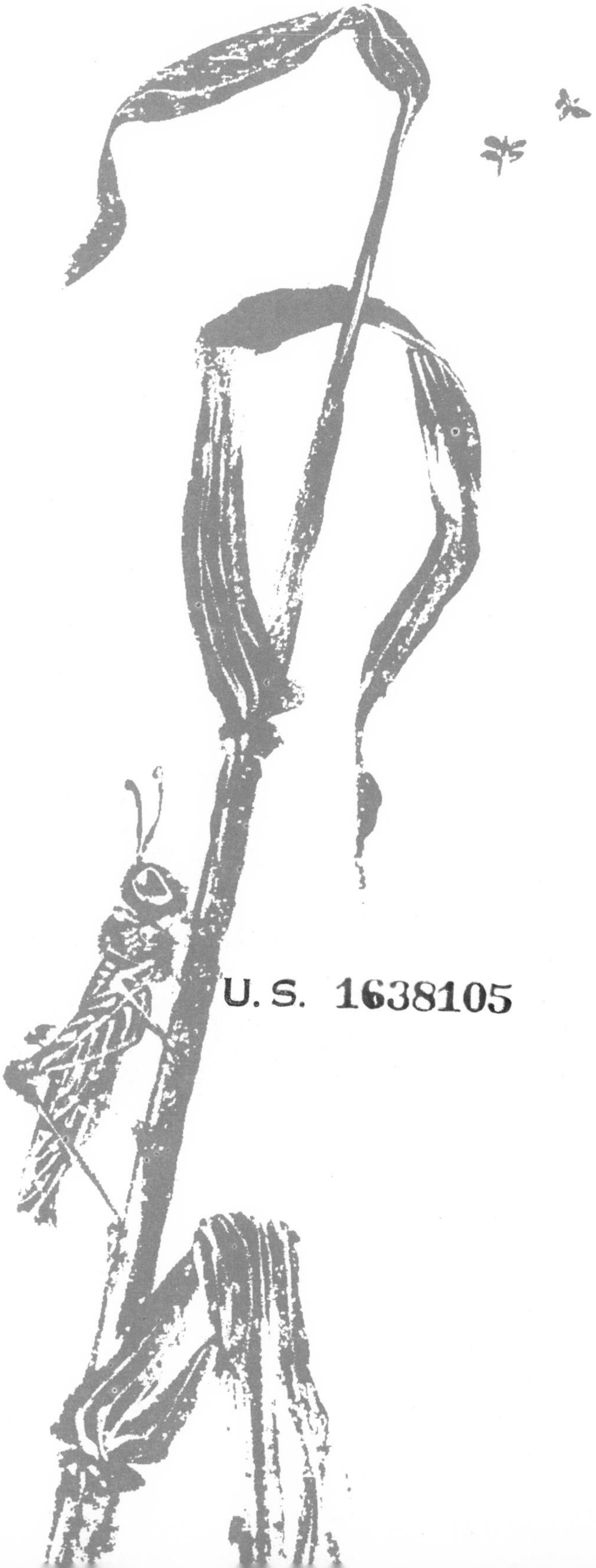

No matter where you live
You use grasses
Every day.

Grasses are important
To you
And to all people.

Indians
Learned to use grasses
In many ways.
Dried grass
Made a smoky fire
For sending up
Smoke signals!

Indians braided sweet grass
And dried it,
Then packed it
In with their clothing
To make their clothes
Smell sweet.

The Apaches in Arizona
Lived in a wikiup,
A round hut
Made of layers
Of dried grass.

And the western Shoshone
Collected tule rushes
To make their special rafts,
With one pointed end,
So they could travel
On the rivers.

While the Hopis are famous
For coiling dried grasses
In beautiful designs
To make trays and baskets
To hold food
And to carry things.

The Paiutes of Arizona
Wove grass into trays
To collect seeds
And gather insects
That they ate.

If the early settlers
Of this country
Had not found grass
Their animals would have died
For lack of food
And they, too, would have starved
Before they ever settled
The United States.

They stuffed their mattresses
With dried grass
To make their beds
Softer.
The brooms they swept with
Were bundles of grasses
Tied on a stick.

And the children
Played with dolls
Made for them
From corn husks.

Even today,
Grass is very important.

Cows eat grass
To give milk
For cream
And cheese
For you.
There are many kinds of grasses.
Chickens eat the seed of some grasses
To lay eggs
For you.
Song birds need seeds of other grasses
For food
So they can sing
For you.

So do horses
Need grass,
And so do pigs . . .
And sheep . . .
And you.

You eat grass seeds
For cereal–
Oats and rice,
Barley, corn, and wheat.
And these seeds make flour
For baking bread
And cake.

wheat
sugar
cane
corn
rye

Grass is planted for food
But we also plant it
To soak up the rain
So we won't have floods.
Without grass
The earth would become
A dust bowl
Under the hot sun.

If you live
Near the seashore
You know grass is planted
On the dunes
To keep the sand from blowing away
In the high winds.

And grass makes a home
For millions of tiny creatures—
Mice and birds,
Rabbits,
Frogs and crickets.

In Hawaii grass was used
To make hula skirts,
And huts to live in.
And a steep grassy slope
In Honolulu
Has been used
For many years
For an ancient
Hawaiian sport —
Ti-leaf sliding.

You pick a ti-leaf,
Then climb up the hillside,
Sit down on the leaf,
And go sliding,
Speeding
Down the grassy hill!

Eskimo legend says
That the Tlingit basket
Was first made by the Sun,
To hold his wife and children
So he could lower them
To Earth.
From them, man learned
To weave these baskets
Of grass and spruce roots.

Different patterns show
Which baskets are
To carry water,
Or berries,
And which are dishes for food
And for special ceremonies.

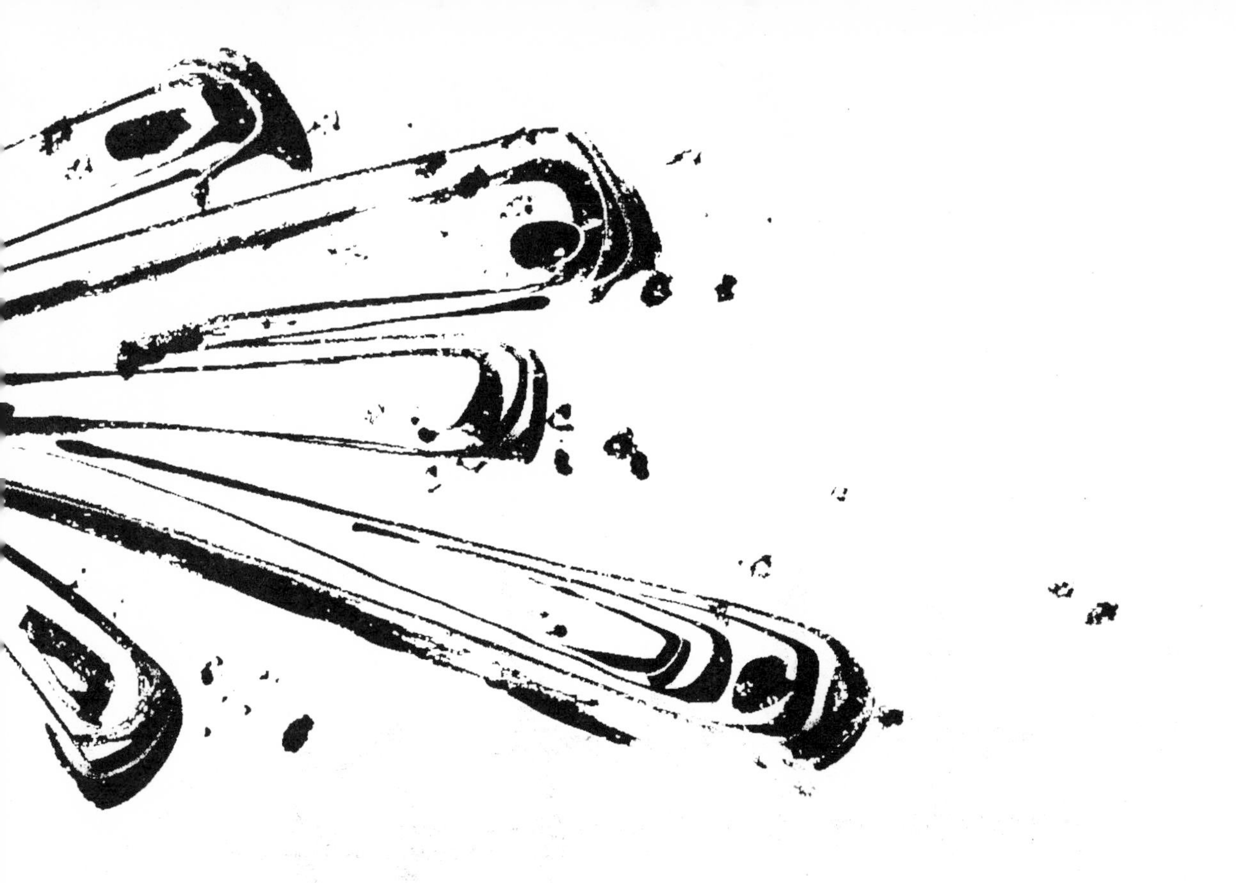

At the end of summer,
Eskimo women gather armloads
Of fine long grass
To twist into thick pads
To stuff into their boots
To keep their feet warm
Against the frozen earth
They walk on.
And the chewy roots
Of cotton grass, sedge, and horsetail
Are collected for winter food.

Did you know
That some grasses
Give an oil
Called citronella
That keeps mosquitoes away?

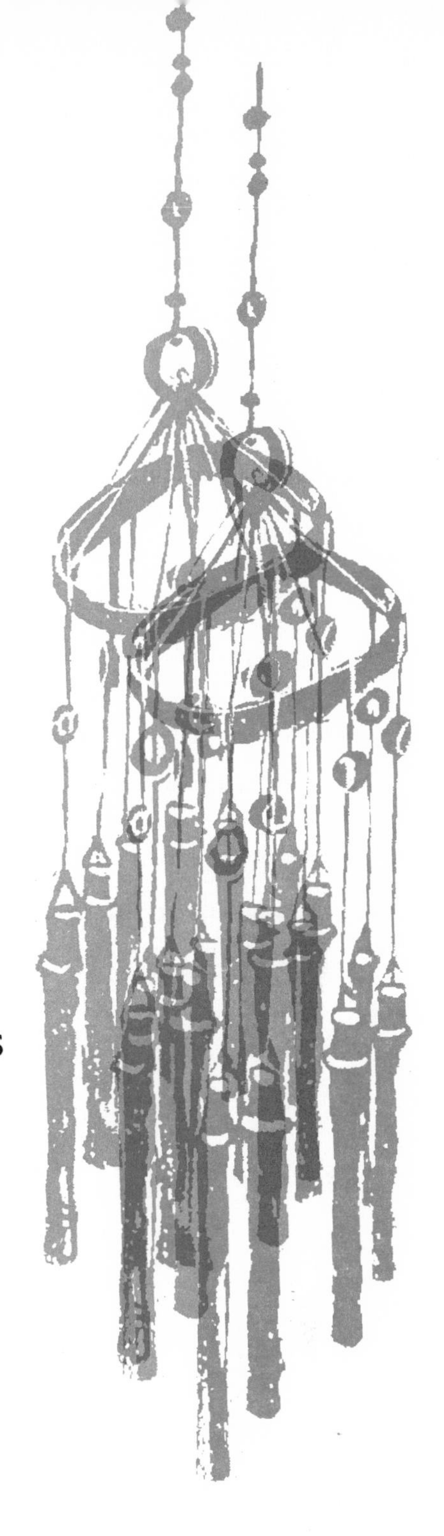

In tropical and subtropical places
There is a grass
Called bamboo
Used for furniture
And fishing poles,
Blowguns
And elephant traps,
Wind chimes
And walking sticks.

Bamboo makes good fences
And stockades
Because its branches grow
Straight out,
Crossing from one stalk
Toward another
To form a dense thicket.
And because it is hollow,
It can be used for pipelines
To carry water
From one place to another.

Bamboo can be split
And woven into nets
And hats.
Its slender stalks can be
A pretty umbrella handle
Or the polished stem
Of a tobacco pipe.

Some kinds of bamboo
Are eaten . . .
Fresh, like asparagus,
Or pickled in vinegar.
Some seeds of bamboo
Are eaten like rice
Or made into a kind of beer.

So grasses are used
For feeding animals
And people like you,
As well as for lawns
Tennis courts
Golf courses
Croquet fields
Archery targets
Window shades
And wallpaper!

You can even have fun with grass–
Making your friend giggle
By tickling his neck
With a long blade of grass,
Or going on a hayride,
Sliding down a haystack,
Making ropes for lassos
And to swing on.

You can run barefoot on a hot day
Through the cool green grass
Or look for a special grass–
A four-leaf clover–
To bring you luck.

Or you can make a whistle–
If you hold a blade of grass
Between your thumbs
And blow hard!

1 2 3 4 5 75 74 73 72 71